Investing Wisely

Long Term Strategies to Secure Investments and Shield Your Finances

By
Fhilcar Faunillan

Fhilcar Faunillan

The information provided herein is stated to be truthful and consistent, in that any liability, in terms of inattention or otherwise, by any usage or abuse of any policies, processes, or directions contained within is the solitary and utter responsibility of the recipient reader. Under no circumstances will any legal responsibility or blame be held against the publisher for any reparation, damages, or monetary loss due to the information herein, either directly or indirectly.

Respective authors own all copyrights not held by the publisher.

The information herein is offered for informational purposes solely, and is universal as so. The presentation of the information is without contract or any type of guarantee assurance.

The trademarks that are used are without any consent, and the publication of the trademark is without permission or backing by the trademark owner. All trademarks and brands within this book are for clarifying purposes only and are the owned by the owners themselves, not affiliated with this document.

Table of Contents

INTRODUCTION.....................................6

Chapter 1 - What Exactly Is An Investment?...9

Chapter 2 - Things To Consider Before An Investment Decision...13

Chapter 3 - How to Invest Wisely 29

Chapter 4 - Financial Strategies To Ensure Investment Security 45

Chapter 5 - Keys To Financial Success...53

Chapter 6 - Things An Investor Should Always Remember 66

Chapter 7 - Tips On Being An Investor And Being............................72

More Financially Secure 72

CONCLUSION.......................................77

INTRODUCTION

Dear reader, I would like to give you my sincerest gratitude for downloading and purchasing the book, *"Investing Wisely: Long Term Strategies to Secure Investments and Shield Your Finances."*

This book is for keeps. I would like to congratulate you in deciding to purchase the book that will help you in the future and will definitely help your future. This book contains everything you need to know on handling money especially on different investments that you are venturing into or you would want to venture in the future. You will find in these book proven steps and strategies that would guide you in making the right and critical choices on where to put your money.

Say that you are an average working individual with some extra cash on hand available for disposal. There are many options in which you can do with your money. You can save it on your own and put it on a safe somewhere in your home. Yes, the money would be there and probably safe but it is idle. It would not grow, and sooner or later you would have to use it. Another option would be to deposit it in banks. Unlike the option of keeping your extra cash inside your house, you would earn some amount if you deposit your money in banks because your deposits would earn interest rates. It is a fact that depositing your money in banks is better than saving it on your own but there are still some catch attached to it like reserved requirement and other financial terms that banks would use. If you would go around and ask successful businessmen on how they do it, they would always tell you that the key to their success is good investment. Investment is the best thing that you can do with your money. Implementing and deciding on really good opportunities is the secret of really successful people in the business world.

The real question now is when to know if a certain investment is a good one or something that would go down the drain. In investing, there will always be some risks. If you want a bigger return then you should not be afraid to face bigger risks too. So, congratulations in buying this book for this will help you open your mind and learn more on knowing which investments is worth it.

This book would also give you some life tips on how to secure your finances and on ensuring the security of your investments. These tips, strategies and steps that are all provided in this book would guarantee you a more stable financial status in the future.

Thank you again for purchasing and downloading this book. I hope you have a great time reading it!

Chapter 1 - What Exactly Is An Investment?

If you would consult the Merriam-Webster dictionary, it would define investment as "the outlay of money usually for income or profit." In other words, it is a capital outlay. It is the outflow of cash in your account towards the inflow of another's. This is the time when you put money or lend your money to someone who really needs it, like someone venturing into a new business, in hopes that they would pay you back in the future at a certain profit. In layman's term, investment is when you lend your extra money to someone who needs, maybe because they would undertake into a new business or property, and in return, they would pay you in the future at a profit.

In economic sense, investment is the purchase of a certain property right now which is not to be consumed but to be used for future use in hopes of gaining profit or income. An example of this would be the building of a factory or a manufacturing which would produce goods. Another example would be the investment that we do when we go to school or enter a university. Yes, we spend money on books, tuition fees, miscellaneous fees and other stuff that needs money, but at the end of the day this is an investment since it would help us go the distance by having a really high-paying job in the future.

On the other hand, when we talk about investment in a financial perspective, it is all about the purchase and sell of stocks, bonds, real estate properties and other types of securities. A security is any type of financial instruments (i.e. stocks, bonds, bills, etc.) that represents an ownership position, or a creditor relationship or rights in a certain corporation. Corporations or the Government issue these securities when they need to borrow money from the public who have extra cash. The public or the lenders on the other hand, will be repaid in the future at a profit.

With the presence of hyper competition and economic crisis, a lot of people do not know where to put their money. Many individuals are going broke, some are losing their jobs and few are unsatisfied with what they earn. This is the reason why people should learn how to invest wisely and take care of their financials. The following chapters will teach you how.

Chapter 2 - Things To Consider Before An Investment Decision

In a world full of uncertainties and risks, the best thing to do is to think of your actions and make a thorough evaluation before implementing it. You will never get exactly the same result that you are hoping for, but at least evaluating your actions before doing it would give an extra cushion for errors. The probability that you make errors would be minimal and the chances of success would be more likely.

Here are some things you may want to consider before taking an investment decision:

- **Investment Objectives**

Investment objective is the goal that you would want to achieve with your investment. It answers the question "Why did you invest?" and "What is the purpose of your investment?" Of course, the number one answer to these questions would be to gain profit or to earn more disposable income. The other factor that concerns this objective is time. How much time do you have to achieve that goal?

Your overall outlook on the trading game is your investment objective. You should know what your goals are so that you can make the accurate trading decisions in the future. There are three major investment objective- safety, income and growth.

1) Safety

There is no such thing as zero risk when it comes to investments, but there are some investments that have smaller risks compared to others. So what are the safest investments available out in the market? The ultimate safety net that we can use our investment funds into would be through the purchase of government-issued securities or through the purchase of high-grade corporate bonds from the market's top performing companies. These two types of securities are arguably the safest securities available for purchase because it contains smaller risks compared to other securities while receiving a specific rate of return.

As an investor, always remember that the safest securities can be found in the money market. The money market is a kind of financial market (the other being capital market) where financial securities with short maturities and high liquidity are being traded. Securities being traded in the money market include Treasury Bills, commercial paper or banker's acceptance slips, and certificate of deposits. There are also some securities being traded in the money market that will provide the investor with a fixed income, and these are government bonds like municipal bonds and corporate bonds. Of all the financial securities mentioned, government bond is the most risky. Always remember that the higher the risk, the higher is the return. So to compensate to the higher risks that these corporate bonds have in them, they would offer you a larger yield than Treasury Bills.

As an investor, you should always remember that there will always be risks when it comes to money matters. Yes, it is true that government-issued bonds and high quality corporate bonds are considered as some of the safest securities available in the market but on the other hand, there will always be junk bonds which offers you a higher yield of maturity and a higher default risk. They are sometimes called as non-investment grade bond because of the high uncertainty of having a return. So, be very careful when investing in money market. It is not right to conclude that corporate bonds are always safe; you should be very critical and observant to a certain security before risking your money with it. At the end of the day, we can say that money market is really safe.

2) Income

"The greater the risk, the greater the return." This should be your mantra. This should be the foundation of your investment goals. If you want to invest in the safest securities in the market, then you should keep in mind that these safest securities offer the lowest rate of yield or income return. So if you want to earn more, then you should be willing to a sacrifice a certain degree safety. If safety decreases, the income return or yield would also increase while if safety increases, the income return or yield would decrease.

As a potential investor, you should know that bonds are classified according to investment grades. Those that have the highest grades are called AAA bonds followed by AA, A, BBB, BB, B and so on. In order to increase returns or garner a higher yield, one must take risk and invest in corporate bonds or preferred shares rather than investing in government-issued securities. It would also give the investor a higher return or yield if they choose to invest in securities that have lower investment grades. BBB rated bonds are assumed to be the security that offers you the higher return or yield compared to bonds with higher grade ratings but carries more risk. Junk bonds, on the other side will give you the highest possible income return but at the greatest possible risk.

3) Growth

Go around and ask people the reason on why they keep on investing. They would all tell you that they engaged in this trading game because they want to earn more. What investors want is to grow their capital or to have capital gains. There is a capital gain when a capital asset's value increases which gives it more worth than the amount that you have used in order to purchase it. In return, you can sell that higher asset in its higher price which would result into gaining more. The gain will only happen once you have sold your asset. However, do not forget the existence of capital loss which happens when an asset's value decrease making it worth less than the time that you have purchased it. When this happens, there are some options in which you can choose from. You can either sell your asset now while your loss is still small or you can wait for the asset's value to appreciate again. The latter is a better choice if you project that the market would do better in the future, but if you have forecasted that it will only worsen, then sell your asset already while your loss is still minimal.

Capital gains can be short term which is one year or less, or it can be for a long term which is more than one year and should always be claimed on income taxes. Long-term capital gains have lower tax rate compared to regular income. This is done in order to encourage businessmen and other people to engage more in entrepreneurship and investment which are good for the overall performance of the economy.

Capital growth is mostly associated with the purchase of common stocks which represents an ownership in a certain corporation which usually offer lower yields but a wide room for increase in value. This is what makes the common stock trading game as the most speculative of all trading since the increase or decrease of a certain asset depends on what will happen in the future.

Those explained previously are three of the major investment objectives that many entrepreneurs have. There are still some investment objectives like tax minimization and liquidity. An investor may want to pursue certain investments in order to lessen the burden on his tax deduction. Many would invest on assets with lower tax rate as an investment strategy. On the other note, many of the securities that were mentioned before are not so liquid or their marketability percentage is quite low which means that they cannot be easily sold and converted to cash. Liquidity and returns are also reversely related. If you want your assets or securities to become more liquid, then you have to sacrifice a certain level of yield or return.

As what we have discussed in the different investment objectives, the advantages of one come at the expense of another. If you want safety, then you should sacrifice your yield. If you want growth, then one must sacrifice return and safety. Choosing which investment objective is suited for you all depends on one's perspective, whether he is risk aggressive or risk adverse.

- **Risk Tolerance**

Risk tolerance talks about on how you handle and balance your fear for financial loss with your desire to see your money grow. Looking at past trends, those investments that tend to go up and down or are more risky offer the biggest gains in the long run.

In order for someone to become successful in achieving his or her goals, one must invest in some riskier assets such as stock. Knowing that stocks would be more susceptible to market fluctuations and would offer lesser income than other types of assets, please also know that it offers long-term growth potential. Of course, a wise investor would know not to invest all of his money in a risky asset. An investor should always keep a part of his money on safer investments like deposit accounts, savings accounts and money market securities.

It is up to you whether you want to be aggressive or conservative. Risk aggressive individuals are those who are not afraid to bet their money on risky investments that offer higher returns while risk conservative people are those individuals that tend to wait and observe before entering the market.

According to a study conducted at the University of California, women are wiser and better investors compared to the male species. The reason behind this is the fact that men tend to become too confident in putting their money on risky assets.

• **Invest in a Diversified Portfolio**

Always remember that you can never get rid of risk in any kind of investment. What you can do however, is to reduce this risk by allocating your money in different financial instruments in different companies and industries and sometimes, in different countries. Its aim is to let you have the optimal returns by holding assets in different locations that would react differently to the same happening. Many professionals would say that diversifying your investment plays a major factor of reaching financial stability and long-term financial goals while minimizing the risk attached with it.

Imagine that you are holding a portfolio of airline stocks. Then say that a major airline accident happen making passengers cancel their flights and many airline employees to quit their job. The result of this is that airline stocks' share price would definitely go down. However, if you also have invested in railway stocks, then only a portion of your portfolio will be affected and not the whole. There is also a great chance that railway stocks' share price would appreciate since passengers would shift to trains as an alternative form of transportation.

Asset allocation does not guarantee that you will no longer face risk though. It will only help you reduce and manage the risk that is caused by the volatility of the economy and the market.

- **Watch Out for Investing Costs**

You can never get rid of cost when investing. It will always be there. Costs are forever. What you can do is to minimize it and keep it low. The lower your costs, the greater share you can harvest in your returns. To have an even greater share, one must control his or her taxes.

Always remember that the higher the costs of a certain investment would affect the portfolio's growth in a negative way. Costs also eat the return that the investors should receive creating a gap between the market return and the actual profit the actual investor actually earns. It is also proven that lower-cost mutual funds tend to perform better than those funds that cost more over time.

Tax on the other hand is a certain type of cost that you can never take your eyes off to. It can significantly affect your returns. One possible way to reduce this tax deducting cost is by allocating your assets to tax favorable accounts.

Before considering in investing in mutual funds or exchange traded funds, always consider the sales charges and fund expenses into consideration.

- **Auto Pilot**

If you are new at this investing game and you are not fairly sure whether to keep on investing or wait some time before entering a transaction then maybe setting up an automatic system that would ensure that you invest regularly is for you. Think about it, you can set up a system wherein it would arrange an automatic transfer of a certain amount of money from your bank account to a mutual fund per month.

Just like every investment plan, this does not guarantee you that there will be profit or there will be no profit loss since this strategy involves a continuous movement of investment. An investor should always check if he still has the ability to purchase such assets at a certain period.

Chapter 3 - How to Invest Wisely

"I think my money is not safe in the market. I probably should just keep it." This sentence summarizes the conclusion that a lot of people are thinking ever since the devastating blow that the 2008 economic crisis have caused to the financial status of many individuals. People are traumatized as they watch their 401K stocks being sold as a 201K stocks.

These days, people are investing again. Business portfolios of different entrepreneurs are starting to grow again and the market is gradually increasing every day that passes. If you want to start investing or would want to invest again, there are some things that you should absolutely know before letting your money come into play.

Here are some things you definitely should know before investing:

1. Diversify

We have discussed in the previous chapter how important it is to diversify your assets. But only few people really know on how to diversify wisely. Here are some tips on how to.

➢ *Mix your assets.* It is not wise if you own a hundred stocks of a certain company or a hundred thousand stocks of only one company and nothing else. You need to invest on stocks of different companies on different industries to really be diverse. To put it only a really nice scale, it is also a good thing if you invest in different types of financial instruments like stocks, bonds and bills.

➤ *Time Preference.* Your portfolio should not only contain different asset classes, it should have in it different financial securities that have different appreciation time lines. This is often taken for granted by most investors but is really a critical part of it. This is important so that your assets would not suffer from downside surprises at the same time. Say that there was an unpredicted economic crisis, if your assets have different time line appreciation then not everything would be affected. Yes, you will still be affected in a negative way since it is an economic-wide crisis, but your fall would not hurt that bad compared to what would happen if your assets are keyed to only one timeline.

➢ *Diversify your Investment managers.* You have already diversified your asset classes and your appreciation time line. One last thing to remember is to have more than one manager. Humans are all very complicated species; we do not know someone completely. It is human nature to be selfish, so if you only have one manager to all of your diversified assets, then you are exposing yourself to another type of risk which is human nature. Your manager can steal from you, ripped you off and take off carrying your portfolio with them.

These are just some of the things you should remember when diversifying. To sum it all up, you should diversify in every level.

2. Create a Financial Roadmap

Before investing, especially if it is your first time investing, calm down, take a seat and evaluate honestly your financial situation. This is the first step to a successful investment in the future. You should first figure out what are your goals and you should be able to measure your tolerance towards risks.

3. Evaluate Your Risk Tolerance

All investments include different types of risk. They may have different degrees, but risk is always there. If you intend to buy different types of assets, then it is important for you to understand that there is a possibility that you will lose money. As tacky as it may sound, investment is a game. It is a gamble that you may win or lose. If you are able to accept the fact that there will be times when you would lose some even if you invest in the safest of all the assets, then you are good to go.

4. Always have an Emergency Fund

A smart investor always know that it is always a good idea to set aside a certain amount of money for sudden emergencies like unemployment or another world-wide financial crisis. This is also a good thing when your investments do not pay off.

5. It is Okay to Engage in Insider Trading Legally.

If you have gathered important piece of information about the market or a certain company in a legal way then you can use it on your own advantage. There is nothing wrong if you have learned this information through your own hard work or through luck. In fact, this is the only time when you can definitely won against the market.

However, be very careful. Do not do this if the company is about the company that you are working for or where your spouse is working for. Also, do not do this if you have an obligation to a third party. In addition, if you learn this information to someone related to you or someone who can gain something from your trading, be cautious for you may be violating SEC rules that covers trading on non-public information. If you there are some level of uncertainties, talk to a lawyer.

Do not think that you cannot trade based on non-public information. The truth is, you can and you should. Just exercise some caution when doing so. Having knowledge that others do not have will give you an upper hand.

6. Read your Quarterly Financial Statement.

You should keep track and read your quarterly statement for you to be able to keep track on your financials. Many people do not want to do this especially if the market is down. They think that it is so ugly; it makes them feel poor and stupid. You should read your financials to know your standing. If you are suffering from loss, this should not cause you to panic. Rather, you should keep calm and think of your next move. Above all this, the most important reason why you should keep track of your statements is to know your fees. Believe it or not, some brokers and funds take advantage of the fact that most people do not read their statements and will raise fees in hopes that the investors will not notice.

7. Rebalance Your Portfolio Occasionally

You should always rebalance your portfolio to your original asset allocation mix. By doing this, you will be ensure that your investments would go back to a comfortable degree of risk and would not emphasize one asset more than others. Many experts would advise investors to rebalance their portfolio on a specific time interval like every six months or annually.

8. Evaluate the Value of an Entire Company

It is important not only to know the current price share of a certain company; it is wiser if you know the value of an entire company. By doing this, it prevents you from overpaying a certain company. It also provides with more room for comparison. It serves as a standard for comparison for other alternative assets.

9. Evaluate Your Reason for Investing in a Company

Before investing, ask yourself what is your in investing in this particular company. Was it because your friends with the owner or a certain employee, was it because of your relatives or somebody pushes you to it or is it because of profit? It is not a smart idea to invest in a particular company just because fell in love with its products and employees. Every good investor knows that paying too much for an investment even in the best companies will always result to a lousy investment.

Always make sure that no heart is involved when making investment decisions. Always make sure that the only reason why you are investing in a certain company is because of its fundamentals. The fundamentals of a company cover its profit, current price, management, credibility, performance, etc. There should be no strings attached when implementing an investment decision, everything should be based on hard, cold facts. If you think that a certain stock is undervalued, walk away.

10. Be Aware of Investing Costs

A lot of people pay too much when investing. It makes them spend more and earn less. These costs may eat your possible profit and destroy your portfolio. If you do not know how to control all of these costs, then you should reconsider investing at the time.

Here is a list of the four major fees that you pay for:

➢ **Taxes.** When your adviser tells you your gains for a certain time interval, he may be talking about your earnings before tax (EBIT). Here's the catch, those are still tax deductible. You will never go home with this EBIT inside your pocket. What you can take home would be your earnings after tax. This shows that you should know beforehand how tax rates would affect your investment and you should be able to anticipate changes in the tax codes.

➢ **Brokerage Commissions.** This is the type of fee that you pay to your broker every time you buy or sell a certain security, especially stocks. Most of the time, this is in a form of a standard amount that would vary depending on the volume traded or the amount spent. Always remember that the lower the brokerage fee, the better it is.

➢ **Advisory Fees.** These are charged by brokers and mutual funds. This fee is based on the size of your portfolio. You may think that this fee will not cost you a lot but these add up immediately. In some down years, there are times when you would pay more fees than what you are earning. There are also some flat years where your income equals to your fees that you would end up not gaining anything.

➢ **Inflation.** This is the major killer of them all. If the inflation is actually larger than your gains, then you are actually losing money rather than gaining them.

11. Reduce your Cost

Now that you know these different fees that can totally destroy your portfolio, the next thing that you should know is in how to minimize these costs. Here are some effective ways:

➤ *Consider Investing on Retirement Accounts.* There are a lot of retirement accounts that are tax-favored. You should be wise enough to use this for your advantage. This would allow you to avoid tax legally in the future which would allow you to save a lot of money.

➤ *Beware of Changing Costs.* Just because you invested in a low cost security does not mean that it would change. There are times when costs would change. This is caused by the entry of new competition and products in the market.

➤ *Find the mutual and index funds that have the lowest costs and invest in them.* This seems like an easy thing to do, but many people take this for granted and overlook this. A small difference in the percentage of what you are going to pay can be a big thing if it all adds up in the future.

➢ *Capital Gains over Income Taxes.* You should be paying capital gains and not income taxes when it comes to your investments. An account which generated sales a lot also pay high taxes. You can reduce this cost by investing on passive funds and long-term investments. Capital gains taxes are lesser compared to income taxes.

➢ *Find those Inflation-Protected Securities.* An easy way to not get affected by inflation is to engage in TIPS which is a short term for Treasury Inflation Protected Securities.

12. Do Not Try and Beat The Market.

Always remember that you can only beat the market if you engage in insider trading or if you are damn lucky. One is illegal and the other is almost impossible to do. You cannot beat the market, you can try but you will end up getting disappointed. You can guide and help yourself though on how to gain based from trends and investment advice. The good news is that you do not have to beat the market. Your main goal in investing is to be able to have enough money to sustain you in the future. Also, another thing to remember about the market is that sometimes, the returns are not what you have expected.

Chapter 4 - Financial Strategies To Ensure Investment Security

In a world that is so volatile to changes, we need to have a plan before engaging ourselves to things that would affect us not only now, but our future too as a whole. Investment is among these things. One should have a game plan in investing. One should not just keep on investing without proper knowledge, briefing and strategy up on his sleeve.

There are different types of investing techniques; here is a list of them:

1. Allocation Management

➢ *Fixed Asset Allocation.* Fixed asset allocation is long-term commitment to whatever mixed investments you are having right now. It does not matter whether the market is rising or declining, you stick to whatever percentage you have in every asset class. This is a classic example of "regardless." Regardless of the fact that there is a shift in the market value of whichever asset you are holding, you would continue to hold that asset and would not change anything.

➢ *Dynamic Asset Allocation.* Unlike fixed asset allocation, dynamic asset allocation is an active way of investing that all depends on market timing. This means that you can change or your investment representative can change your asset mix depending on the current status of the market. This asset allocation management strategy is one way of taking advantage of the assets that are performing well in the market and is one way of preventing yourself from major downfalls in the future.

2. Buy & Sell Strategies

➢ ***Buying at a margin.*** This happens when there is an opportunity in the market but you do not have enough money to finance yourself. What you do is you borrow money from your dealer or broker in order to have the purchasing power needed for that certain security.

➢ ***Buying Options.*** This is just some basic terms you have perhaps learned in undergraduate school, but it can become your strategy to successful entrepreneurship. This is the right to sell a specific stock at a specific price to someone, at a specific time. However, this is a right and not an obligation. If you think that you would not gain if you do this, then you can choose not to push through with this. There are two kinds of options: call and put. Call is when you have a right to sell stocks while put is when you have the right to purchase stocks.

➢ **Day Trading.** As the name suggests, this kind of trading happens when you buy a certain stock today and also sell it at a higher price before the day ends. In other words, it is simply trading (buying and selling) of financial instruments within the same day. Although this kind of trading has been exclusively participated in by financial professionals, bankers and firms, this has been open to all at present. Stay-at-home traders have been day trading stocks, currencies, various futures, and options to name a few with the advent of margin and e-trading.

➢ **_Market Timing._** This is one kind of investment strategy wherein you based your actions on trends, past data and history. You can also base your investment decisions depending on the volume, market price and economic data.

➢ **_Hedging._** This is something you do when you do not want to deal with the volatility and unpredictability of the market. This is when you offset a security's position by engaging with a contract someone that states that you will buy a certain stock at a certain price at a specific time in the future.

➢ **_Shorting._** This is one kind of buy and sell investment strategy wherein you would borrow money from your broker or dealer in order to have the ability to buy a certain fund or security. This is different with buying at a margin in a sense that you should know that it must be bought back later and returned to the broker.

➤ ***Indexing.*** This is a little bit conservative way of investing wherein a portfolio of an individual tries to mirror the stock index performance available in the market.

Be cautious though. These strategies are a little bit complicated and quite risky. It is best if you have a financial adviser if you are really not an expert on these things or at least try to have a better understanding of these stuff before engaging in it.

3. Philosophy

➤ ***Value Investing.*** This is a strategy wherein you buy stocks of companies that are being sold at a discount. You later hold it for a long time. If the company has a credibility and the needed fundamentals to raise its price, then it will not be long till the market realizes its value and make the stock price. Then, this is the time where you can sell your shares at a profit.

50

➢ ***Growth Investing.*** This happens when you look at trends of the market price of different companies. This growth investing happens when you buy shares of companies whose prices are going higher based on the economic data that you have gathered.

➢ ***Top-Down Investing.*** This happens when you evaluate a certain security from a general level to a more specific one. First you examine the overall performance of the security based on the sector, industry and country that it belongs to. Then you examine the next level until you have narrowed it down to individual companies.

➢ ***Bottom-up Investing.*** This is the opposite of top-down investing. This happens when you first evaluate the overall health of a security based on the company. You first examine the company's performance in the market, its credibility, customers, employees, managers and financial reports. Then you take it to a more general level such as the industry. You would evaluate if the industry that it belongs to is a rising or a declining one. Then you examine the country or sector in which the company is located. You evaluate if the location would fall like having an economic crisis or any type of phenomenon that would disrupt the rise of the economy.

Chapter 5 - Keys To Financial Success

You might think that there is a perfect time to start trading and investing. The truth is, there is no perfect timing. This might sound as a cliché since we hear it all the time, but as an investor, you should not wait to get started. Start immediately. This will give you more time to build experience and examine the market in applications. Another thing that you should consider is the time value of money. The money that you have right now is worth more than the money that you will have tomorrow. Why? It is because of the logic of time value of money. When you have extra income right now, invest it right away since it can already earn some interest in it and make it much more than its value yesterday.

Also, as much as investment is a game of money, it is also a game of the mind. It is all in the mindset of a certain individual. The calmer you are, the better decision you can make. Should you stumble and face a certain crisis, stay calm and think about your future actions. Never ever panic.

Always know that nobody is born as a really good investor. It is an acquired skill. It would get developed as time goes by and through experience. It is easier than you would think. If other people can do it, then you can do that as well.

To make things more systematic, here are some things that would lead to financial success in the future.

1. Have a plan

Having a plan is knowing what you like. You should have your goals and objectives and you should know what to do in order to achieve them. You should know the reason why you are saving and investing. It might be because you want to buy a house, car, life insurance, health insurance, education, or for retirement. The best thing to do is to have a list and then decide which of these goals would be your priority. Also, you should set a time interval when you would reach these goals. You should have a time line to everything so to that you can do the right actions in order to achieve these objectives.

2. Always Keep Track of Your Statements

This would be the start of everything. This is the starting point of your journey to financial success. When evaluating your financial situation, you should be really honest with yourself. Do not sugar coat or try to hide really ugly statements and sheets because it is your money that you are looking. No matter how small or ugly it is, accepting the fact that you only have that much is an important step.

You can also make this step easier by making a list of what you own and what you owe. You should be able to compute your net worth manually. You can start by getting a piece of paper and fold it in half. On one side, write everything that you own or all of the assets that you have while on the other side, write everything that you owe or all of your liabilities. To know your net worth, add everything listed on the asset side and do the same on the liabilities side. After this, subtract your liabilities from your assets. If your assets have more value than your liabilities then you have a net income or a positive net worth. On the other side of the coin, if your liabilities are greater than your assets, then you are at a loss or a negative net worth.

If you have a negative result to this, you should not be discouraged. You should be able to motivate yourself to try harder and flip the tables to the other side by aiming in making it as a positive number. If you follow a plan, then, sooner or later, everything would be alright.

The best thing to do is to always do this occasionally in order to keep track on your financial stability. Another thing that would help you control your financial situation is by keeping track of how much you make and how much you spend within a month. If you have a family, track down how much you and everyone else who is making money is earning every month and do the same on your expenses every month.

3. Do Not Invest All of Your Money

This has been said repeatedly, but as a potential investor, you should always remember that there will always be some risks attached to an investment. So, the best thing to do is to keep a portion of your extra income for yourself or for your family which would serve as a cushion should something bad happened to you in the future that would affect your finances just like a sudden death or unemployment.

What other people do is that they allow their banks to automatically get a fraction of their salaries every month. This would save the hassle and it would be more efficient. There are also some plans depending on which company which automatically deduct money plus the tax that you should pay. This is most common to retirement plans. If you are working, ask your company if they have this.

4. Know Your Taxes

In school, we have been taught to focus on the returns that your investments would give you. What they failed to teach us is that the important thing is not what you earn, but what you get to keep after taxes have come in the way. If you keep on investing on funds that are not tax favored, then you are not earning what you deserve. As an investor, here are three of the major taxes that take a toll on your earnings:

➢ *Income Tax.* This depends on how much you earn annually. Always keep in mind that the higher your income is, the higher the tax that you have to pay. A typical high earning individual usually has an income tax that would rise to about 50 percent of their total earnings. This is due to the combined federal and state income taxes.

➤ *Short-term Capital Gains.* If you are going to sell an investment that you have for less than a year, you should be aware that you can be charged with short-term capital gains tax which is usually in the same percentage as the income tax.

➤ *Long-term Capital Gains.* This is the opposite of short-term capital gains. If you hold your fund for more than a year, you can be charged with long-term capital gains tax which is about 20 percent.

5. Structure a Great Portfolio

Experts always say that it is best if you would allocate your assets in diverse accounts. There is more to this than just investing in different accounts. Parking your money wisely and dividing it in the best mix available out there is the most important skill a successful investor should have.

Many know that there is a need to diversify, but what others do not know is how to. The basic thing that you should do is to diversify by choosing different asset classes like stocks, bonds, real estates, equity and others. Then you should avoid putting your money in one asset class. Say you have this certain amount for the bond market. What you should do is to avoid putting all of your allotted money in one company's bonds. You should look at other industries and other companies. You can also diversify up a notch higher by diversifying in a global level. You can look at different markets, countries and currencies. The last thing to do, which is also mentioned in the preceding chapters is to diversify on different timelines. By spreading your money, this would reduce the risk that you may have and may not cost you anything.

When you try and diversify your assets, there will always be some corresponding costs. The question is how will you reduce your cost and keep more of your earnings? The first thing that you can do is to defer taxes. You should always find the best tax-free or tax favored accounts available out there and use them. You should also try and stay away from short-term capital gains. Why? This applies perfectly if the account you are holding is tax-deferred since you have to hold an account for at least a year and a day in order to qualify for the long-term capital gains rate. You should also try and consider index funds. Index funds is like a basket of companies that would only charge you if the index of the fund changes. The good news is that this rarely happens. This is a nice thing since this would allow you to avoid paying taxes. This is a clever way to earn with you paying the taxes. As long as you do not sell anything, and as long as your money is in the fund, it will keep compounding. Lastly, you should be cautious of mutual funds. Investing in mutual funds might be attractive but if you keep it on your portfolio for too long, you might be paying higher income taxes in the future. You should only keep mutual funds for a short period.

6. Make Your Money Grow

There are two major ways on how to make your money grow. One is by working hard to be paid by money. The other one is by letting money work for you. Basically, it is working for money and money working for you.

The first way to make your money grow is by following the basics. After you graduate, you find a job and get paid. That is it. You can earn more by having more than one job at a time or by getting promoted. However, letting your money work for you is an easier task. When you let your money earn for you, it only means one thing: having a steady pay check. This is the best way to earn more, by using your extra cash. The logic is like, people would you pay you by letting them borrow your extra cash. If you are working and you have an investment, then it only means more cash for you. You can earn a lot if you let your money work while you yourself are working.

Another way of letting your money work for you other than investing is buying a certain property that has the ability to increase its value over time and sell it at a higher price than your face value. One main example of this is on real estate properties. You can buy a land now and sell it five or ten years later since most lands usually appreciate their value over time.

To iterate, the best way to make your money grow is by working and letting your money work for you.

Chapter 6 - Things An Investor Should Always Remember

➤ It is proven by a lot of experienced investors and experts that the stock market's intrinsic value increases every six weeks. This increase is also only about one percent. Everything else out there is irrelevant.

➤ You should not be too anxious and keep on investing. You will lose your money faster than a bullet train travel. There have been some studies that have shown that people who trade most earn the lowest returns.

➤ Even purchasing securities issued by the top companies in the world may be considered as a bad investment if they are purchased at the wrong price.

➤ There is no perfect time when investing. There was a time when the highest-income generating stock was bought during the great depression. Sometimes, you earn more when you face risk.

➤ You should not think that you invest on really complicated and hard to understand stocks that it will give you the highest returns. There is no such thing as that. Stocks are stocks. The simplest form of stocks may sometimes give you the greatest returns.

➢ Most successful investors have three secrets for their success. One is compound interest, no matter how small your interest is, it will still multiply because of compounding. Another one is time. Always remember the time value of money. That the money that you have right now is worth more than the money that you will earn tomorrow. Last is patience. They are able to wait and sit around. They do not panic when their investments does not make money on the first try because they know that they have the ability to recover.

➢ Do not believe in everything that you read in the papers or over the internet. When experts forecast that a certain event will happen in the stock market, there is a fifty-percent chance that it will happen. So, there is also a fifty-percent chance that it will not.

➤ You should always have an answer to this question, "How long will you remain invested in a certain stock?"

➤ People could sometimes mix-up trend with a winning investment. There is a difference between these two. A trend may compose of different companies on the same industry. It would be wise for you if you study each company fist before investing in them because not all of them would guarantee you a winning investment.

➤ If it seems like you cannot find a really good investment, then it is okay. There is no problem in that because what matters is spotting those really awful investments. It is best to know which investments would be bad for your financial health and avoid them rather than trying to find the best investment out there.

➤ Before the global economic crisis happened, everyone sort of knew that it was bound to happen. The same thing will happen in the future if another crisis is about to happen.

➢ As what have been discussed again and again in this book, always remember that the main antagonist with your investment would be the stocked up costs and expenses which would seriously eat your potential earnings. The good news is there are some commission-free, tax-favored and low-cost accounts available out there. If you find one, seize it.

➢ Annuity can help you reduce your cost from taxes.

➢ Inflation is a bane to your investments. Always check this one. You may not notice it now but your long-term investment may actually be losing you money instead of earning.

➢ Always be careful when you try to invest in places with different currency. I have this instructor once who told us that he invested in a foreign country. But since his own country's currency depreciated, he ended up losing money even if the stock price of the company abroad in which he invested in have increased. He lost it, when he tried to convert the foreign currency into his own country's currency.

➢ If you are in the market for a long-time then do know that most market movements that happen daily are caused by short-term investors. Try your best to ignore what they do.

➢ The most important thing that you should answer is "Are you in for the long-run or just for a while?" You should know how long you will be investing. If you are there to earn an extra income for a while or you are there until you retire. This will change your perspective on how you will be playing the game.

Chapter 7 - Tips On Being An Investor And Being More Financially Secure

> ➤ *Diversify.* It has been said again and again but it is so important that this concept would stay in your mind. This should be the mantra of every investor since this could save a life. And that means literally.

> ➤ *Always have a ready to access funds.* There are some opportunities that come

along in a snap of a finger. You should be prepared when these types of opportunities come along because they also go away in an instant. It is easier if you have readily accessible funds than taking much time in looking around for money by borrowing from others or liquidating some of your accounts.

➢ ***Do not always invest in a hot tip.*** Just because someone tipped you that a certain account would earn you a lot, you should not readily invest in that account without prior investigation and study of that certain account's background. Even if it came from your best friend, lover, relatives or boss, one should not invest in a fund without research and analysis.

➢ ***Never buy funds based on impulse.*** If you see a new fund readily available in the market, think first before investing. Also, only buy stuff that is really with significance in the future. Do not buy a car just because you like its design or a sales

73

person talked with you into it. This would let you save enough money that you would be able to use if the right opportunity arises.

➢ **Try to avoid having debt.** This should be a goal of everyone who wants to have a stable financial status in the future. Everyone should, as much as possible, avoid debt especially those debts that compound through time.

➢ **Track your income, expenses and analyze them.** If you see and realize that you spend more than you earn, then you should change the way you live. You should also do something about it, either you minimize your expenses or find something that would let you earn a higher income.

➢ **Try to create an emergency fund.** This should amount to at least three to six months of your income so that it would be enough to back you up in times of emergency.

➢ **Have fun.** Do not stress yourself about those little things. Live your life while you are still young. If you lost in a trading game, do not stress yourself to death, there will always be another day to make a comeback. You should however, find a balance. Use your time and asset wisely.

➢ **Have the right connections.** In the business world, it is nice to have friends or acquaintances that are interested in the same field as you do. This would make your life a little bit easier since they can help you, guide you and teach you some steps, ways and easier habits on how to invest properly.

➢ **Do not forget about your family.** Remember why you are doing this. Why do you want to earn more? Is it because of you? Is it because of your wife or your kids? Remember to do this when investing. It would make you make better decisions.

CONCLUSION

I would like to congratulate you for being able to reach the last part of the book. I would also want to say thank you once more for choosing to download this book.

I do hope that this book has helped you in understanding what it would be like to become a wise investor and a good handler of your hard earned money. I hope that this has helped you in achieving your goals and that it has served its purpose to you.

This book will serve as your guide as you wave your way into the financial world of reality. However, always remember that this is your guide, you can choose to follow those that are written here or you can choose to bend some and create your own. It is on your own discretion whether you would do this or not.

The first thing that you should do is to earn money that you can invest. However, do not spend everything that you earn all at once. You should be able to save some for future emergencies or expenses. You should always be mindful and responsible enough to at least save a portion of your income as an emergency fund since it will serve as your cushion. You can earn faster and save faster if you have more than one source of income. You can work two jobs at a time if you want to. Then if you already have the enough amount of fund to enter an investment, then do it. If it works out, you can earn more by having more than two sources of income.

Then, if you already have established a certain amount ready for usage, you can apply everything that you have learned in this book into use. You can let this book guide you, discipline you and tell you the right way to do things. As what I have always said, do not be afraid of a little setback. Everybody loses some time. The important thing to do is to always remember to do better the next day. Nobody is perfect, even the richest persons and the most successful investors have faced a little bump in their lives. You have just to be critical so that you would not be creating the same mistakes over again.

I wish you nothing but the best in your future days. I hope that you become one of those successful investors and become financially stable.

Finally, if you enjoyed this book, then I'd like to ask you for a favor, would you be kind enough to leave a review for this book on Amazon? It'd be greatly appreciated!

Thank you and good luck!